MEN WHO FEED PIGEONS

Selima Hill grew up in a family of painters on farms in England and Wales, and has lived by the sea in Dorset for over 40 years. She received a Cholmondeley Award in 1986, and was a Royal Literary Fund Fellow at Exeter University in 2003-06. She won first prize in the Arvon/*Observer* International Poetry Competition with part of *The Accumulation of Small Acts of Kindness* (1989), one of several extended sequences in *Gloria: Selected Poems* (Bloodaxe Books, 2008). *Gloria* includes work from *Saying Hello at the Station* (1984), *My Darling Camel* (1988), *A Little Book of Meat* (1993), *Aeroplanes of the World* (1994), *Violet* (1997), *Bunny* (2001), *Portrait of My Lover as a Horse* (2002), *Lou-Lou* (2004) and *Red Roses* (2006).

Her latest collections from Bloodaxe are: *The Hat* (2008); *Fruitcake* (2009); *People Who Like Meatballs* (2012), shortlisted for both the Forward Poetry Prize and the Costa Poetry Award; *The Sparkling Jewel of Naturism* (2014); *Jutland* (2015), shortlisted for both the T.S. Eliot Prize and the Roehampton Poetry Prize; *The Magnitude of My Sublime Existence* (2016), shortlisted for the Roehampton Poetry Prize; *Splash Like Jesus* (2017); *I May Be Stupid But I'm Not That Stupid* (2019); and *Men Who Feed Pigeons* (2021), shortlisted for the Forward Prize.

Violet was a Poetry Book Society Choice and was shortlisted for all three of the UK's major poetry prizes, the Forward Prize, T.S. Eliot Prize and Whitbread Poetry Award. *Bunny* won the Whitbread Poetry Award, was a Poetry Book Society Choice, and was shortlisted for the T.S. Eliot Prize. *Lou-Lou* and *The Hat* were Poetry Book Society Recommendations, while *Jutland* was a Special Commendation.

Selima Hill

MEN WHO FEED PIGEONS

BLOODAXE BOOKS

ISBN: 978 1 78037 586 1

First published 2021 by
Bloodaxe Books Ltd,
Eastburn,
South Park,
Hexham,
Northumberland NE46 1BS.

www.bloodaxebooks.com

For further information about Bloodaxe titles
please visit our website and join our mailing list
or write to the above address for a catalogue

Supported using public funding by
ARTS COUNCIL
ENGLAND

Cover design: Neil Astley & Pamela Robertson-Pearce.

Printed in Great Britain by Bell & Bain Limited, Glasgow, Scotland, on
acid-free paper sourced from mills with FSC chain of custody certification.

ACKNOWLEDGEMENTS

Acknowledgements are due to the editors of *Poetry London* and *The Poetry Review* where some of these poems first appeared.

CONTENTS

The Anaesthetist

The Beautiful Man with the Unpronounceable Name

Billy

Biro

The Man in the Quilted Dressing-gown

Ornamental Lakes Seen from Trains

Shoebill

THE ANAESTHETIST

The Anaesthetist

Again my mother powders her nose,
again the tall anaesthetist explains,

again she doesn't hear a single word
because she is distracted by his eyelashes.

The Banker

Where the swimsuit digs into her skin,
the woman's body glares an angry red

that shimmers in the sunshine like the wine
shimmering beside the burning banker.

The Care Worker

The residents are old and so in love
it's all the same to them if he's chubby

or permanently stoned or if it's him
stealing stuff from their bedside lockers.

The Chauffeur

Whenever I see him, he's asleep,
squeezed inside his caravan like dough,

with at his side a little china wheelbarrow
containing a selection of sweets.

The Childhood Sweetheart

Nobody lives here except sheep.
We spend the days standing in the river

eating sloes and freshwater shrimp.
He is one, and I the other, gender.

The Classics Teacher

By the afternoon he was gone.
What I hated most was the suit:

we are dressed in flimsy summer dresses;
he is sweating in a tweed suit.

The Cousin

The day my cousin draws me the gazelle
and tries in vain to teach me how to wink

he's crushed to death by the one-eyed bay
that liked to poke its head inside my window.

The Dancer

The only thing that cheers him up is gloves.
He keeps a vast collection in his attic.

The man himself is still the shyest man
it's ever been my privilege to dance with.

The Dentist

Every day I watch him go to work,
complete with little hat and pigskin gloves.

On Sunday afternoons he cleans his car
and slips a chocolate penny in my pocket.

The Doctor

The handsome doctor rises from his desk
and holds my head as if it were a cabbage;

as if he has, as indeed he does have,
a perfect right to come so close to me.

The Doctor of Philosophy

That the tiny doctor of philosophy,
quivering with joy like a fly

quivering with joy above a wound,
is said to be a man is irrelevant.

The Driver

The man in the refrigerated lorry
containing the dismembered one-eyed bay

is going very fast but not so fast
he doesn't know he should be going slower.

The Duke

The grizzled duke who walks beside his mother
was born to hold her bony hand at funerals.

The Entomologist

The entomologist is so tall
he's balanced on his rock like a giraffe

that someone's dressed in highly-polished climbing-boots,
the shiny leather laces pulled tight.

The Ex

Celeriac is not the same as celery;
a boyfriend's not the same as an ex;

a goldfish is no longer a goldfish
when floating on its side in its tank.

The Farmer

He stares across the fields like a horse
that doesn't know and doesn't need to know

that there's another world beyond the valley
made of glass where horse-deniers live.

The Father

He runs across the beach with a beach ball
and falls about laughing he's so happy

and ends up on his back completely helpless
underneath a heap of sandy children.

The Film Director

To anyone who's got any sense,
it's all about my *fear of being loved.*

The Finn

At first I really thought he was dying
(he looked like Jesus he was so thin)

but gradually we settled into this –
this drifting in and out of being here

and being nowhere else except the paradise
of not yet knowing how his life will end.

The Friend

Because he's very close, but not too close,
and not too far away, because he's real,

when he takes my hand I close my eyes
and tremble like a mass killer sobbing.

The Gardener

He treats her like a doormat in a dress
that loves to get as filthy as it can

and if she doesn't pull herself together
she'll end up upside-down on the compost heap.

The Geek

The geek's become the geek because God
was curious to see what geeks can do

but now that He has seen what they can do
He goes upstairs and reinvents the mammoth.

The Great-grandfather

The man I've come to read to doesn't move.
He's like a man who doesn't exist,

a man who can't begin to understand
how much I value my not being seen.

The History Teacher

Anyone who wants him will find him
chasing after balls at the tennis courts

where tennis players play without knowing
they'll never wear their hair in plaits again.

The Man Who Sits in Saunas

The man who sits in saunas sits in saunas
not because he thinks he's losing weight:

he needs to sit in saunas to compose himself
while waiting for the end of the world.

The Married Man

The married man, as someone who has chosen
to do what he is told, to eat fruit,

to take up squash and to abandon squash,
is lying in a bed full of tissues.

The Mathematician

He lets me share his bed on condition
we never cuddle, and we never do.

The only thing he loves is mathematics
and mathematics has exhausted him.

The Monk

His eyes, like shrimp, or broken fingernails,
glitter in the dark which is tonight

the closest thing, alas, to a wife.
She holds him in a lap he can't touch.

The Nurse

The tired nurse looking for a vein
is being very careful for no reason –

unless we call care itself a reason.
He's inching up my arm like a bee.

The Opera Singer

I'm sent by train to a large house
in which there lives a melancholy Chow,

a woman with red lips, and a man
who spends the days teaching me to row,

and every evening, followed by the Chow,
to help the woman with the red lips

lay the polished table in the dining-room
where nobody will dine except me.

The blisters on my hands are like slugs
crawling in and out of my fingers.

The Painter

His hair is thick and lustreless like horsehair.
If I kneel down, he lets me touch it.

He lives and dies in poverty. In time,
each painting will cost more than a yacht.

The Patient

The patient in the pin-striped pyjamas
slides across the ward like a door

that leans against the nurse as if to say
please can she be sparing with the truth.

The Photographer

What I like about him is the fact
that everybody thinks he's a failure;

that he and I know he is not:
we know his speciality is *puddings.*

The Poacher

Curiously thin, with ginger hair,
the poacher is transforming himself

before my very eyes into a fox
that throws me toffees as it shoots by.

The Retired Solicitor

The man who lets me ride on his horse
has got two arms but only one hand

with which he likes to stroke the giant horse
on whose back I learn to be afraid.

The Sailor

He had a few women, a few kids,
but left them all behind like old clothes:

he never stops anywhere long enough
to benefit from knowing where he is.

The Son

She says that he was forty, and obese,
and on the day she suffocated him

she says she asked her son one last question:
Can't you just be normal? But he couldn't.

The Supply Teacher

He drives a car that must have cost the earth
and waves to little kids he didn't know
and strides into the classroom in a blazer
singing at the top of his voice
as if it's not a crime to sing like that;
as if it's not a crime to wear a watch
as big and heavy as an aeroplane;
as if he isn't perma-tanned for nothing.

The Tennis Coach

Is it true that sharks avoid virgins?
And do I look as ugly as I feel?

Should a man who's overweight be punished?
Can a person live without revenge?

Can a dying kitten smell of angels?
Have a million dustmites got it wrong?

Is the New Active Zip Plunge Superbra
available in more seductive colours?

And is it true that if I love the tennis coach
I need to make is *absolutely clear*?

The Tennis Player

Although the blinding sun is beating down,
the tennis player never stops playing –

and everybody's hoping that the reason
is nothing like as bad as they think.

The Tractor Driver

The other girls wear ribbons in their hair
and stay indoors where it's warm and clean

but I prefer to ride in the trailer
behind the man I beg to call me *Sheep*.

The Treasurer

When the matron goes to find the tea-room,
I slip away and plant my first kiss
deep inside the collar of the Treasurer –

and we are still in shock when the matron,
having fondly hoped it would reform me
to *represent my school*, sees her mistake.

The Uncle

Every time I beat him at chess
everybody marvels! (Chess is easy –

it's the other things that are difficult.
Like sitting on his lap, for example.)

THE BEAUTIFUL MAN WITH
THE UNPRONOUNCEABLE NAME

Standing on His Doorstep

The goose with yellow legs like yellow egg-yolks
standing on his doorstep's only me

dreaming I'm a goose because a goose
hasn't got a clue what it's doing.

A Happy-looking Man

A happy-looking man, for a change!
And that's what's made me come here in the first place –

I'm fed up with the men in my life
who seem to think happiness is irrelevant.

The Beautiful Man Whose Name I Can't Pronounce

I can but it's so beautiful I don't.
I prefer to think it's unpronounceable,

to go to bed and think of him as fruit
glimpsed at night by someone who is lost,

who walks for many days, weighed down by maps
and dictionaries and old pronunciation guides

until she's so exhausted and confused
she can't pronounce the name of where she's going to,

never mind the name of the fruit
into whose fat cheeks she dreams she's biting.

Never Go Upstairs in the Daytime

Never go upstairs in the daytime,
never kneel down beside a bath

in which a man with an unpronounceable name
is singing to himself and his sponge.

In the Tiny House

In the tiny house nothing happens –
only me imagining my breath

tickling him like breath made of eyelids;
only me saying I must go.

The People Who Still Call Themselves My Loved Ones

The people who still call themselves my loved ones
wouldn't even know me if they saw me –

I've disappeared, I've gone, I've left no trace
except the footprints of a large bear,

the kind of bear who finds a small child
and drags her off into the undergrowth,

never to be heard of again –
or, if she is, she's said to be mute.

The Toes of the Woman I've Never Met

The house is full of upside-down bicycles
among whose spokes I'm terrified of meeting her,

of falling at the freshly-polished toes
whose pinks and blues will twinkle like fresh bedding-plants.

A Café We Could Go To

The beautiful man with the unpronounceable name
says he knows a café we could go to.

I shake my head and catch the train home
where nothing will make sense anymore.

God's Gift to Wasps

I've realised that he's one of those people
who go to cafés all the time, with everyone,

and doesn't know that cafés are God's gift
to men and women wasps who like to party.

A Cup of Tea

He asks me if I want a cup of tea.
I shake my head and run to the station

to spend my days trying to figure out
why I didn't simply say *yes*.

The Face of the Woman I've Never Met

The purse she carries smells of the purse
in which I kept the sickly-smelling powder-compact

needed for the noses of the dolls
who sat in rows waiting for the suitors

they knew would never come. Her perfect face
shimmers in the mirror like Antarctica.

Never Even Hope

Never even hope. Bow out now.
Bow out backwards in the sort of trance

in which you can't stop bursting into tears
in spite of, or because of, a sensation

of being lost inside immense bouquets.

A Woman, a Cyclist and a Teapot

All it boils down to is this:
a woman, a cyclist and a teapot;

the woman (me) saying she must go,
the cyclist's large and medium-sized smiles.

The Nose of the Woman I've Never Met

She drives her nippy car, she toots her horn,
she smiles left and right and turns her nose up

at those who leave their dusty rooms by moonlight
in dusty boots with beetles in their hair

and as she drives her nippy car she curses
anyone she feels like cursing.

Hating Me Would Be a Waste of Time

Hating me would be a waste of time –
hating someone who is so uncouth

she spends her time falling over bicycles
and doesn't even moisturise her cuticles.

What Kind of a Woman Am I?

What kind of a woman am I not to speak?
Not to say a word, to be struck dumb,

to back away like a newborn toothpick
that hasn't learnt to pick what it must pick?

The Word *Marriage*

She's a woman. I'm a woman. Women
are not here to rock each other's boats.

But why say 'boat'? Why not say 'marriage'?
Am I frightened of the word 'marriage'?

Baby

I'm begging him to stop but he won't,
he carries on regardless like the flies

crawling in and out of the baby
whose tiny silver bracelet bears my name.

I'm Never Going to Think of Him Again

I'm never going to think of him again
or let my mind linger on the elderly

sitting in their bungalows and thinking
life is much more brief than people think.

Bicycles and Tricycles

For him who stockpiles bicycles and tricycles
my heart is breaking – which is pathetic:

I've spent my life avoiding men like that,
their halls so full of bikes you can't think.

Krasznahorkai, Djokovic, Leghorn

Surely adults always say *something*
but all I did was stand there and say nothing.

On the train, to calm myself down,
I wrote a list of names I can't pronounce

to see how many I could spell, a list
of other people's husbands and a chicken.

They Said It Would Be Hard

They said it would be hard but it's easy
living not with him but with a sofa-bed,

so cow-like in its reassuring cosiness,
if not the way it can't, or won't, moo.

Eating Potatoes in the Shed

When he asked me out, was he secretly
hoping I would say I couldn't come?

Could he see that all I want to do
is hide inside the shed and eat potatoes –

not only with the gardener but the insects
that tiptoe up and down our necks like curates?

The Cake

It never takes my hand or asks me questions
but sits in silence on its outsize plate,

emerging only rarely from its icing
to quail at the touch of my knife.

European Night Train Guides

Like a beetle on her best behaviour
setting off across old *European Night Train Guides*,

I didn't understand where I was going,
that tying myself in knots would get me nowhere –

not that beetles tie themselves in knots,
they never tie anything in knots.

Spearmint Freshbreath Mouth-freshening Beads

Never leave the house without your mouth-freshening beads;
never wear a dress that doesn't fit;

never be alone with a cyclist,
even one, like him, without a knife;

never go upstairs in the daytime –
and never think you love him when you don't.

I Hear or Think I Hear on Moonlit Nights

I hear, or think I hear, on moonlit nights,
the furious tinklings of a million bells

and see, or think I see, his wicked grin
flashing like the gold and silver necklaces

of millions of hyperactive tricyclists
tricycling out of sight as fast as they can.

BILLY

My Mother's Extraordinary Hair

I started telling him about her hair –
how long it was, and white, and I was saying

how, when I was a child, I was scared of it –
when, seeing he was getting bored, I stopped.

What It Feels Like To Talk To Him

When I talk it feels like I'm talking
to somebody who doesn't speak English,

somebody who's new to this country
and doesn't understand what's going on.

The Plateau Phase

When we were at school my friends and I
could never figure out what it was

and whether men experienced it as well.
Now I know a man, I can ask him.

Stone

He's like a stone – inasmuch as stones
never smile. Even charming stones.

Crab

I pray he doesn't offer me the crab.
I pray he doesn't even mention it.

Jelly

Just as he, to me, seems very hairy,
I, to him, must seem very shiny,
like a jelly shining on its plate.

Raging Torrents, Soaring Peaks

Unmoved by raging torrents, soaring peaks,
he's busy looking forward to the cakes.

Rain

He won't admit it but he hates the rain.
If he's in the rain without a hat

he keeps his mouth resolutely shut
to stop himself from bursting into tears.

I Try to Please Everyone

I try to please everyone. Of course I do.
And everyone tries to please me.

Everyone, that is, except him
who's sick of always having to be charming.

The Woman with the Broken Leg

After spending all the afternoon
beside the woman with the broken leg

I feel the glow that only kindness brings.
He glares into his tea: *She's an idiot.*

Honey

I do confide in him, but only rarely,
and when I do I always regret it:

he acts as if I'm smearing him with honey
in the dark with my bare hands.

Sheep

Like a sheep coughing on a moor,
I say I'm sorry fifty times a day.

He, however, doesn't feel the need
to say he's sorry, even if he is.

The Sun in All Its Glory

He hates the rain. He even hates the sun.
When the sun comes out in all its glory

he scuttles into corners like a spider
that suffers from a fear of being loved.

His Childhood

His father wept. His mother was a beetle
who talked all day on the telephone.

Romance

I'd love to be romantic but I'm scared
I'm going to make somebody cry.

Restaurant

He's talking on his phone and as he talks
I'm writing down a list of all the things

somebody can do in a restaurant
while the other person's on the phone.

The Long Wait

He's nearly two hours late but I don't mind.
I don't mind a bit. I like waiting.

When he's maybe four or five hours late
I still won't mind. Or that's what I'll tell him.

Skinny-dipping

I lead him to the place. Peering in,
he only says *It looks rather dark*.

The Married Couple

As we pass the couple holding hands,
I'm praying he's not thinking what I'm thinking.

The Gents

I watch him wander off to the Gents.
And once again I hope he'll take ages.

Other Members' Towels

He knows the other members by their cars;
I, however, know them by their towels.

One of them has got a towel with Elvises
printed on one side, for example.

Expensive French Cheeses

He brings me some expensive French cheeses
made from the milk of tiny human mothers

fed on hare in isolated villages
where little girls grow up to be beatified.

Brandy Snaps

Watching him eat brandy snaps, I'm learning
not to keep expecting to be heard.

Everyone Is Watching

Everyone is watching me and wondering
if somebody sitting on her own,

even though she's clean, and a woman,
is in fact a *serial killer.*

Friendship

Someone told me once, to my surprise,
it's possible to have *enough friends.*

I don't know if it's true or not and anyway
I don't know what a friend even is.

As We Leave

As we leave, I hear someone say
I've known that guy for seventeen years

and never heard him speak before! I smile,
having been the one to whom he spoke.

The Compliment

He complimented me and I was pleased.
Maybe I'm less confident than I think.

Prawn Cocktails

I don't know what they are but I hate them.
I hate them without trying them, like skiing

and anything to do with skiing – skis,
salopettes, skiing instructors,

strawberry-flavoured snow – with one exception:
avalanches is my favourite word.

Me and Juan Martín del Potro

It's not as if I'm Juan Martín del Potro
steadily improving his tennis.

Being nice and trying to be nicer
doesn't work. It only annoys people.

Doll

I try to keep my mouth shut, like a doll
strangling herself to death with her own pigtails.

A New Pair of Fleece-lined Gloves

He doesn't seem very well today –
wearing gloves, not finishing his cake –

but anyhow I'm learning that it's best
not to show I notice these things.

Sitting as Still as I Can

Every time somebody is ill
they teach me the lesson I'm so bad at

of making them as comfortable as possible
by *sitting as still as I can.*

Baby

All he wants to do is lie down.
All he wants to do is be remembered.

All he wants to do is be a baby
like a baby born before its time.

The Red-haired Swimmer

Everybody loves the red-haired swimmer,
even him. He loves her most of all!

His little face lights up like a night club.
It seems a shame to say she can't swim.

The Tea Is Cold

The tea is cold. The parking is expensive.
The women nag. Everything is hopeless.

Fancy Cakes

The man whose tea is never hot enough
is peering at the row of fancy cakes

that may look good to everybody else
but not, as usual, good enough for him.

Pain

He moves as if he's, not in pain exactly,
but wary, like a man dressed in glass.

Teabag

I squeeze the teabag hard against the mug.
He isn't listening to a word I'm saying.

The Jolly Sailor

With his usual discontented look,
he buys a postcard of a jolly sailor.

Shopping

He loves to shop. At the little café
he asks me what I want and I decide

I would like Maltesers. (He would like
a proper garage, with a garage drive.)

My Life as a Pair of Crocs

I try to look both earnest and adorable
like surgeons' crocs before they're sprayed with blood.

The Extra-large Crab Sandwich

He orders me an extra-large crab sandwich
I do my best to look pleased to see;

I do my best to do what God would do,
if God exists, and if He eats crab.

The Sea

He's sitting with his back to the sea
facing the car park, in a bobble hat.

I myself am facing the sea.
I thought the sea was the whole point.

On the Beach

On the beach he shouts at my dog.
I say *Don't shout*. He buys himself a bun.

Kindness

Some of us like to be kind
and some of us are tired and can't be bothered.

Trolley

He's like a patient propped up on a trolley
who doesn't want to know he's going home;

who can't, or won't, respond to the arms
trying and failing to help him.

Dinner

The man who never smiles always smiles
when anyone asks him to dinner.

Piglets

His head is like a barn full of straw
where piglets go to sleep in warm heaps.

The Surgeon's Ring

He's gazing at her ring and not listening.
He may look half-asleep but he's afraid.

Walking Back to Happiness

I squeeze into the van and start to sing
when all he wants to do is stare at traffic.

Sadness

I think he is embarrassed to be kind,
as I am to be tender, which is sad.

Hollyhock

He calls his neighbours' hollyhock a hollyhock
so I was wrong to think he knows nothing.

Chihuahuas

He smiles at the red-haired so-called swimmer,
he smiles at the red-haired swimmer's dogs

so, yes, the man who never smiles does smile.
I should have said 'who never smiles at me'.

God

The surgeon's got striped hair like a hyena.
Her tiny hands, to my surprise, are cold.

I want to ask her, but I don't know how,
what she thinks of God, and being God-like.

The Brunette

I've never seen the red-haired swimmer swimming
or even paddling. And her hair is brown.

(Some of us like to dye our hair
and some of us do other things instead.)

The Tea Is Never Hot Enough

The tea is never hot enough. The neighbours
never sleep. The bank takes all his money.

Teddy

All day long I tried to make him happy
and, as he wasn't real, I succeeded.

Chickens

He doesn't really smile when he smiles
or even seem to swim when he swims.

The only thing he actually enjoys
is scattering small villagers like chickens.

Pink-and-white Fairy-cakes

The pink-and-white fairy-cakes he's peeping at
look as if they want him to christen them.

Furniture

He wants to be alone with his furniture.
Furniture doesn't bounce around

or ask him endless questions about God
or things like joy he doesn't understand.

Semolina

If he's fed until he can't move
I can do whatever I want.

Buttered Toast

My ancient teddy taught me to be kind.
I made him beds and fed him buttered toast.

But the man's a man and not a donkey
and being kind is never kind enough.

The Warmth of the Knife

He's like a man who's lost in a storm,
who can't remember how to get back home,

who sees, or dreams he sees, a warm knife
levelling the icing on a cake.

Teapot

I bring the tea. He touches the pot.
The tea is never hot enough, he says.

Sand

The tide is going out. As we watch
I can see more and more sand.

I think it's coming in, I hear him say.
It's good he's not an Admiral or the moon.

Midge

He treats me like a midge. In other words
he looks at me and suddenly can't think.

Cupcake

Godforsaken, bald and incapable
of answering my endless boring questions,

he's concentrating on his choice of one,
and only one, little coloured cupcake.

Every Time He Hurts Me I Tell Myself

Every time he hurts me I tell myself
he doesn't understand, he's like a child –
and sometimes that can help and sometimes not.

The Man Who Never Smiles

The man who never smiles never smiles.
However hard he tries, it doesn't work.

Chocolate Pudding

I sometimes think I'm boring him so much
all he wants to do is close his eyes

and tell himself I'm someone rich and famous
who'll make him chocolate pudding and not talk.

His Mother's Dog

It bit him on the nose and she fainted.
Apart from that, he never mentions her.

Table

Familiar, inert, he's like a table
that wants to tell me something but can't.

Poodle

Today he's got a hat on like a poodle
but strides about as if it doesn't matter.

I want to say that's what endears me to him
but maybe it's not true nor ever will be.

The Buffalo

Apparently the cream is from a buffalo
that regularly floats off the ground

which means the cream is holy in some way.
Apparently the buffalo's a saint.

Bucket

He sits beside me like an old bucket
someone's put beside a fire alarm.

What We Need to Think About

Eating cake is all very well
but what we need to think about is money –

money, which is God's way of helping us
tear each other to pieces overnight.

Hand

First I touched the car, and then the coat,
and then the hand, familiar as loss;

a hand that feels cold, that can't be held,
a hand that is the absence of a hand.

Corridor

Disappearing down an endless corridor
piled high with other people's towels,

he seems to care more about his dinner
than whether he will come back still alive.

The Smile

And now he is transformed into someone
who's affable, athletic and redeemed.

Solutions

If I think he's starting to get cross
I leave him to get cross on his own.

I gather up my things and leave him there –
which doesn't solve anything either.

Photographs of Women with Straight Hair

Of all the *'50 World's Most Powerful Women'*,
only one has not got dead-straight hair.

The redhead swimmer's also straightened hers.
I myself have got curly hair.

Ammonia

She paddles in the water with Chihuahuas
as if to say why swim when you can paddle;

she walks along the walkway in stilettos
as if to say why walk when you can totter;

the cakes she bakes are baked by 'little helpers';
the lovely hair, so straight and red, is brown.

In Giant Shorts

I dread the way he shuffles back and forth
in giant shorts as if he looks OK.

The Plan

I ask him kindly if it makes sense.
He replies *Nothing makes sense.*

Him and Me

He never seems to want to explain things.
It never seems to enter his head.

He eats his cake and explains nothing.
Because he isn't me, I suppose.

The Currant Bun

As he eats his bun he should consider
Lester Piggott, who is half his size.

A Person Who Is More Amenable

As I won't eat cake, I suggest
he asks a person who is more amenable.

Armadillo

I call the Audi in the drive 'the car';
I call the cake they call a gateau 'cake';

I call the other women 'she' and 'they' –
but I call the armadillo *armadillo*.

Giraffes

Another person is another person.
He's not supposed to be the same as me.

If I prefer giraffes, for example,
it doesn't mean to say he has to, too.

Battleships

He must be much more charming than I think he is –
he can talk to people about cars,

he can peel eggs, and play Battleships –
but anyhow he doesn't charm me.

My Idea of Fun

I'm wheeling him along in his wheelchair
mile after mile through deep snow

while feeding him chocolate eggs and yodelling.
It's fun for me but not so much for him.

Coffee-pot

I envy him the way he can live with
a coffee-pot encrusted with sugar.

Thirty Murdered Women

Never be alone with a mosquito
and never have a coffee with a woman

who wouldn't be seen dead with a Chihuahua,
who never stops talking about hair –

about the fact that the hair of the murdered women,
in every case, all thirty, was red.

Two Bananas and a Frog

He brings me two bananas and a frog
whose beautiful long legs are black as night,

as dreams of having once been alive,
of finding it's too dark to make it home.

The Good Fortune of the Man Sitting Opposite Me

Everyone's an idiot except him.
Fortunately, he is not an idiot.
He is cool. (Or heartless, as I call it.)

Badger

He's like a badger hunting in the moonlight
who's fed up to the teeth with eating worms;

who doesn't want to think about the future
and doesn't want to think about the past;

who knows he ought to 'live in the present'
but doesn't want to have to live here either.

Mount Fuji

Anything he doesn't understand,
anything he doesn't like, he squashes –

he's like a sack, or a sack-like slug:
the way a slug, in time, can climb Mount Fuji.

Pig

Everyone is more or less the same.
Any minute someone might provoke him.

He moves along like an old pig
a pigman is driving to the slaughter.

My Mother's Car

He'd like to know the make of her car –
but not, please not, the texture of her hair

(how fine it was, how cold, like the hair
on hair-grass or the necks of certain moths).

Oxygen

He's like a man in a long tunnel
who feels his way forward in stiff gloves

through which he finds he feels almost nothing;
who wishes he had brought his canary.

Life and Death

If you changed the film he was watching
to a different film half way through,

it's as if he wouldn't even notice:
life and death is neither here nor there.

I Used to Cry

I used to cry but now I can't be bothered.
I rise above it like the break of day.

Electroencephalographs

He's got better things to do than bother with
someone trying to explain electroencephalographs.

A Normal Person

When he left the house he said goodbye
like a normal person. I thought *Progress.*

His New Bobble Hat

I myself prefer to live with men whose hats
are unadorned by reindeer with red noses.

Prayer

Please can God or someone come and render him
more capable of awe and less flat-footed.

Other People's Noses

Nobody must mention his mother,
his mother's dog, or other people's noses.

(I sometimes think all we've got in common
is our dislike of our respective noses.)

Little Billy

His mother's little Billy bit his nose –
a nose she then compared to the noses

of men and women, even small children,
whose perfect noses little dogs have spared.

Rhinoplasty

One of the young women in the Powder Room
powdering their noses was his mother,

powdering her nose for the journey
to visit her imperfect son's rhinologist.

Golden Sands

We've suddenly found ourselves alone
and feeling all the feelings of the tenderness
we came out here to try to forget.

Hospital

All that really matters is our *helpfulness!*
He forgets how *helpful* we can be.

Propped up on his pillow at the hospital
he doesn't feel helped. He feels miserable.

A Racehorse Called Rhododendron

I don't know if we are or if we aren't.
I don't know if we are or ever will be.

When he's slow like this I can't help thinking
Please can someone send me a Rhododendron.

Sunshine

He and I are sitting on a bench
not knowing if we're *happy* or *not happy*.

I'm not used to being disagreed with
so I am almost certainly *not happy.*

The Duty Doctor

The duty doctor doesn't like the look of us –
him, the patient, me, the patient's carer

into whose freshly-washed ear
she whispers some timely advice.

Profiteroles

We're trying to pretend we're here on earth
to have a laugh and eat profiteroles;

we're trying to pretend we're not ashamed
of knowing we're pretending we don't care.

The Visitor

The person who appears beside his bed
is only me, reborn as a visitor –

whose gift of roses Nurse has snatched away.
Her little shoes recede. Tap, tap. Tap, tap.

Ears

He always looks hard-done-by – like a donkey
but without a donkey's king-size ears.

Mother

My mother's lap was like the eerie dunes,
her hair, the long and windswept marram grass

that cuts you if you try to get a hold on it.
It's best to leave the marram grass alone.

It's also best not to mention Mother
or Mother this or Mother that or mothers.

The Hospital at Night

The patients are adrift on their wards
like dust and sugar in the kitchenette.

The doctor says there's no way of knowing
which of them will pass away next.

Kilimanjaro, Kilimanjaro, Kilimanjaro

I ask too many questions,
why's the orange orange, what's that noise,
who is Offa, how can it be shown
flamingo lilies purify the air?
Who called Kilimanjaro Kilimanjaro,
which is worse, jealousy or envy,
does he agree with the so-called Moral Relativists

that what is right for some is wrong for others
and why do drag queens seem to love the 50s –
mackintoshes, shampoo and sets?
And, by the time I ask him if the doctor
has mentioned *blepharitis*, he's asleep.
His eyes, already small, look even smaller,
defeated, like two pigs in a poke.

BIRO

The Visitor

This person we can hear is my uncle.
He lets himself in via the balcony:
he'll suddenly appear, like a thief,
or like an angel, neither of whom *chat*.

Like a Man Who's Never Been in Love

He's like a man who's never been in love,
who's never been excited about anything,
who stares ahead as if he's made of glass,
with glassy veins and a glass heart.

Rectitude

When my uncle's walking down the street,
his footsteps on the pavement whisper *rectitude*;
when he disappears inside his house,
his slippers on the carpet whisper *rectitude*
and when he's resting, *rectitude*, *rectitude*,
the whispers interrupted by the barking
of Biro, the Hungarian Vizsla.

My Uncle and Me in the Tobacconist's

Does he love me? Certainly not.
But here, to my surprise, a chocolate rabbit,
wrapped in gold, is pressed into my hand.
But soon the smells of chocolate and tobacco
make me feel faint and, as they talk,
I lay myself down on the floor
and nothing will induce me to get up again.
The rabbit takes its chance and runs off.

My Uncle's Drawing-room

My uncle has no past and no future.
In the stillness of his drawing-room
he sits alone, savouring the hush,
like a bullet nobody must touch.

My Uncle's Kitchen

I can't see any food. Only chopping-boards,
a marble slab and rows of tea and coffee-pots.
Beyond the kitchen, in the scullery,
the housekeeper is reading Deuteronomy.
I peer at her like a lone explorer
peering at a body locked in ice.
Then we hear the tinkle as my uncle,
far away, tinkles his bell.
The housekeeper tells me the butler
is *useless as a slug in a cardigan.*

The Billiard Room

Everything in the house is grey,
a muffled, incorruptible grey –
everything, that is, except the billiard balls
shut inside the billiard room like parrots
whose yellow beaks can peck you to death.

My Uncle's Bentley

Very early every Friday morning
my uncle, in a coal-black riding-jacket,
highly-polished, knee-length riding-boots
and snow-white jodhpurs, steps into his Bentley
and disappears down the empty street.
No one in my family owns anything
as priceless as my uncle does: a horse.

My Uncle's Vegetable Garden

Beyond the lawn, beside the tennis club,
he cultivates a vegetable garden.
The vegetables that grow in this garden
seem to have been given, been entrusted with,
a silence only they can understand.
They guard it like my uncle's faithful butler
guards my uncle's fascinating sins.

My Uncle's Blazer

The eight brass buttons on my uncle's blazer
glimmer on his chest as if to say
eternity itself will not be long enough
to scratch, to even dull, their convex gleam.

Newts

Like newts, or Yiddish, say, my uncle's secrets
may intrigue but never frighten me,
they're soft, discreet and beautiful, like newts
I've only ever seen the absence of.

A Housekeeper, a Butler and a Horse

A housekeeper, a butler and a horse.
Has he got no other friends or colleagues?
Nobody. Unless we count the Bentley
tucked behind the automatic doors
of what must be the world's cleanest garage.

Brothers

When he comes it's when his brother's out
and even then he never sits down.
The six brass buttons on his blazer glint.
In his hand, a pastry from the pastry shop.
He's come to talk to Mother about money.

The Baths

My uncle likes to visit The Baths
where people go to sit and dream, like lizards,
or numbers in the depths of mathematics,
lost, at ease, in chanceries of steam;
where people go to tell each other stories
in languages the young no longer speak.

My Uncle's Mother

In the picture you can see my uncle
standing stiffly in a white dress.
His mother's face is hidden by a hat
with, on the brim, what look like ostrich feathers.
She died when he was three, the butler says.
He says she died of *bloodymindedness*.

My Uncle Plays the Piano

He plays for no one, only for himself,
hour after hour, like someone swimming,
from island to island, in the snow.

More than Seven European Languages

According to the cook, my uncle speaks
more than seven European languages –
but who, I wonder, does he speak them to?
And what about? *Horses*, she replies.
And once he rode an ostrich on an ostrich farm.
He was ten. He hated every minute.

Artichoke

The billiard room is silent as the grave.
Nothing moves from one year to the next.
Why is no one seen in the billiard room?
Why is no one seen in the house
except his faithful butler and the cook?
How come he never sees his baby brother
although his brother's living right next door?
Occasionally I'll see him from my swing
carrying a lettuce or an artichoke
towards our garden gate, his blue-grey skin
pockmarked like the ostrich or a handbag.
He walks with care and never looks up.

Poppet

The Polish pastry shop is full of nuns.
They either speak in Polish or say nothing.
The woman who is minding the shop
is teaching them to say the word *poppet*.

Silverfish

He pads along the carpets of his corridors
in leather slippers, entertaining no one
except the moths and silverfish who also
appreciate a house without a sound,
or only certain sounds, such as footsteps,
the music-room curtains being drawn
and music being flawlessly played.

Hotel Wellingtonia

Where the branches overhang the wall
they make a sort of passage where I crouch
and watch the headless neighbours in their living-rooms
moving in and out of sight like guinea pigs
moving in and out of sight in hutches.

Doll

The way he stares ahead as if displeased,
the way he never looks me in the eye,
the way he repositions my doll
as if to say a doll must do no wrong –
my uncle is himself like a doll.
His back is straight, he's cold to the touch,
he never laughs or cries, he never sleeps,
he never speaks until I leave the room
and then he speaks only with reluctance:
like a doll, he is too proud to *chatter*.

The King

Maybe he is someone else entirely,
maybe he is actually a king,
a much-loved king in hiding whose subjects
play the piano faultlessly from birth.

The Illustrated Guide to British Moths

My uncle's face is like a hundred moths
that fly away if anyone says *horse*.

Chocolate Sardines

I must never hear him play the piano,
I must never sip or sniff his tea,
I must never spy on the butler
or covet his tins of sardines.

Vivarium

Every hair, every lash in place
(his ears a little prominent perhaps,
like flaps, or tabs, for peeling back the face
that looks as if no one's ever stroked it,
no one's ever kissed it or fondled it),
like a saint, a vision of a saint,
like a jonquil that distrusts the sun,
he blinks and disappears. Or like a lizard
homesick for a home where nothing moves,
nothing needs to move, the tiny jaws,
hushed and heated, have no need to snap.

When Biro Barks

When Biro barks my uncle frowns: the barks
disturb – and it is easily disturbed –
something that my uncle spends his days
trying and failing to get close to.

Doctor

I want to ask him where his patients are
and why aren't I allowed to see his horse
and does he know the eyelashes of ostriches
are made of feathers, does he know that bats
laugh about his ears in their belfries
and does he think she should have pinned them back.

The Bell

From my perch on top of the wall
I can see my uncle in the breakfast room
eating boiled eggs like a king.
Beside him is the bell because a bell
is perfect for a man who much prefers
to ring a little bell than to speak.

My Uncle's Horse

I must never climb the garden wall,
I must never frighten the cook,
I must never ask a single question,
I must never write what I have written;
I must never age, or be a woman;
I must never find myself alone
wondering what happened to the horse.

Cow

Certain children play on their own –
maybe they've got no one to play with
or maybe they are ugly, or just weird.
I myself am one of those children.
Luckily I've got a cow called Cow,
made of tights, with stiffened cardboard ears,
in whom I can confide because she listens.

The Doctor

From high up in the branches like a hunter
I watch the so-called *Doctor* in his gardening gloves
examining his disappointing gooseberry bushes.
Does he have a different way of touching?
A way of touching that is barely human,
a way of touching how a fish might touch?
His fingers when he passes me my medicine
are scrubbed so clean they feel like the lips
of bony fish in mourning for their ocean.
But what is the opinion of his patients?
And does he even have any patients?
Is he or isn't he a doctor?
And, after my ordeal, does he know
that all I got was one propelling pencil?

Photograph of a Baby

The baby's eyes are framed by heavy lashes;
the ears are like two butterflies, the skin
luxury saloons' untouched interiors.
Even as a baby he looks humourless
and underhand like other people's bathrooms.

Key

Why he needs to see her I don't know
but sometimes he will visit my mother
and sometimes she will offer him tea
but, if she does, my uncle will refuse
and leave the house before he hears his brother
coming up the steps with his key.

The Word *Jodhpurs*

I can see my uncle in his riding clothes
crossing the garden to his garage
and as he disappears he shakes his head
as if to say he can't believe my spelling.

Berries

His touch is like the touch of a bandage,
soft but slightly sinister, or berries,
and being touched makes her feel good
the way it feels good to feel helpless.

Spiders

The doors are closed behind him like felt doors
being closed behind him in felt walls
and on the other side of the doors
he goes to sleep like spiders in felt curtains.

My So-called *Personality Disorder*

He cannot tolerate interruption.
He's like a skilled surgeon under lights,
disinfected, sober and suspicious
of anything that might approach joy.
I tell myself he doesn't know everything.
I tell myself to rise above his citing
my so-called *Personality Disorder*.

What to Wear on Horseback

He knows exactly what to do and why –
what to wear on horseback, for example,
or how to be as charming as a newt;
how to spell discreet and *Bougainvillea*
and what to do with dead and dying psychopaths.

Fathead

When he meets me crashing down the stairs
he looks at me as if to say *Fathead*,
as if to shout, as if to scream *Fathead!*
but no, he's much too dignified, of course he is,
as dignified as a dressed stone.

My Uncle's Bedroom

If I don't sit still my uncle leaves
to spend the evening in his own domain
where nothing moves except the occasional moth
that moves around his bed like a moth
around a moonlit roof-top swimming-pool.

Cheerfulness

The butler, still dressed in the cardigan
with slightly different sizes of button
he wears in bed even in the summer,
is watering the roses with tea.
My mother stands above him on the balcony
polishing her spectacles with silk.
Nobody feels like talking.
Nobody except the ever-cheerful
members of the Lawn Tennis Club
who carry on playing without knowing
my uncle passed away before breakfast.

Ostriches

They run all night like dreamers in a dream
on rock-hard feet while waving giant plumes,
they run so hard they starve, they die young,
not only young but beautiful, like me,
staring at myself in the mirror
while everybody else is at the funeral.

THE MAN IN THE QUILTED
DRESSING-GOWN

His Hairy Ears

He thinks there's someone knocking at the door –
it happens all the time – but there isn't,

there must be something wrong with his ears,
he ought to see a doctor, but he won't.

His dressing-gown really needs washing
but the cleaner 'lost' the other one –

how can someone lose a dressing-gown?
The cleaner goes upstairs. She doesn't know.

The other one didn't show the dirt,
or not so much. But what's that dreadful knocking?

His Semolina

Eau-de-Cologne, he bellows, *eau-de-vie*,
he can call it anything he wants to

and he can dream as much as he likes
and if he wants to sweep about the dining-room

dressed from head to toe in green velour
and feed himself on crystallised angelica

the colour of a parakeet, he can;
or burn his semolina, he can.

His Most Precious Possession

As the person in the grey-green dressing-gown
is once again laboriously explaining

how important *graciousness* can be,
the weary cleaner disappears upstairs,

leaving her employer in the kitchen
cradling his most precious possession,

a teapot – which, like a young lady,
must never be allowed to grow cold.

His Incomparable Picnics

In a world where everyone seems lost,
he needs to demonstrate to his children,

rooted to the spot as they are,
and on the verge of tears, that he himself –

isn't it blindingly obvious? –
is far from being lost; is, on the contrary,

perfectly capable of organising
one of his incomparable picnics.

His Stony Silence

In view of the constant flow of stinking people,
measuring this, pouring that, running,

running headlong to the door and back,
and in and out of his, now stinking, bathroom,

his *current plan of action* is to cultivate
a dignified, if rather stony, silence.

His Slender Ankles

His ankles are surprisingly slender
(or anyway they were) but his legs

have almost given up, they feel moribund
the way a sausage-roll feels moribund,

they'd rather be kept gently horizontal
and never be expected to bear weight.

His Little Rest

It may be daytime but what's wrong with that,
a little rest, at his age, after all,

he deserves a little rest, in bed,
(*on* the bed, not *in* the bed, of course not)

he's going to lie *across* it, like a cat
that needs a little rest to clear its head.

His Missing Spectacle-case

But when he says a *tea* he means a *sherry*,
not too much, someone else can cook,

someone else can read the tiresome books
whose tiny letters might as well be flies,

someone else can deal with the children –
the women who should never have been born,

the men who are not men (he takes a sip)
but celibates who swan around in skirts

while men who know they're men are hard at work
making love in bullet-proof hotels –

someone else can do it, why not,
and please can someone find his missing spectacle-case.

His Passion for Musicals

He looks as if he's falling asleep,
the matted cats all piled on his lap,

but if the cleaner tries to push them off,
or turn the telly off, he attacks her.

His Itchy Fingers

His itchy fingers' fungal infection
doesn't seem so itchy late at night

when cats and foxes roam the darkened streets,
but, like eternity, *affirmed and justified.*

His Curvy Ladies

So here he is, flat on his face,
waiting for a passer-by to rescue him –

and they do, they carry him back home
and up into the bedroom where he tells them

how he met (he whispers a name)
and how he's always liked his ladies *curvy.*

His Dusty Dressing-gown

In order to make out the illegible –
or try to – the illegible hand-writing

of someone he no longer remembers
whose letter he is holding in his hand,

he's screwing up his eyes but, no, he drops it
and reaches for some yellow cake instead

whose dry and indigestible crumbs
join the drifts of grass-seed and fur-balls

that hover round his ankles and his knees
and creep between his skin and the velour

as if the nap itself secretes a dust
whose purpose is to drive him insane.

His Useful Walking-stick

He's carefully manoeuvring his body,
as warm and apathetic as a pie,

towards a small but evil-looking spider
he suddenly whacks on the head.

His Toasty Socks

Although his ankles may have once been slim
that doesn't mean to say they are now:

they swell inside his toasty socks like grubs
that haven't got a care in the world.

His Shaky Hands

In the half-lit, less than half-lit, drawing-room –
beside the coffee table and a box

from which a tissue, like a perfect bud,
impassively unfolds itself and waits

for somebody who's having to hold back
(but even he can't hold them back for ever)

the tears whose fury no one can deny –
her skin-tight fishtail evening-wear is shimmering.

His Love of Opera

The things he used to do and loved to do
he can't do any longer and the lady

he used to love to do them with is gone
so now he is reduced to those acquaintances

who remain alive but know nothing:
most of them don't even know his name!

His Pinks

The sickly smell is so overpowering
he's even being overpowered himself:

he doesn't move, or speak; he just sits there
like a sinking mousse. It's the pinks.

His Starry Nights

Those starry nights when he, or so he says,
danced the fastest and most modern dances,

those wild starry nights that the dancers
used to think would last for ever, didn't.

His Enormous Feet

Scrabble's too much fiddle, all those tiles
cascading to the floor, chinking uselessly,

the tiny numbers, furious arguments,
and what's the point of winning anyway,

can't they understand that all these girls,
all these little *jellies in pyjamas*,

can (he rubs his socks) go *straight to hell*
(he kicks his shoes off and unrolls his socks),

he needs to be alone with his Imodium,
his Viennese slices and the dizziness

that pulls the ground from underneath his feet
even though his feet *weigh a ton.*

His Victoria Sponge

The nice young woman takes him by the arm
and steers him through the doors of the patisserie

to choose a cake she promises to feed him –
to crumble into manageable spoonfuls

and spoon between his lips with a teaspoon –
a promise that is never fulfilled.

His Big Blue Face

Those shuffly, those infuriating people
he used to take no notice of, why would he,

unless they started getting in his way
and then he'd simply shut his eyes and *tread on them*,

grind them underfoot like broken shells,
those shuffly people who have found themselves

stranded in a world where dirty cushions
are piled at their backs, behind their necks,

under cats or stuffed in cars and wheel-chairs,
those shuffly people *now include himself*

and no one knows or cares how much he's hating it
because, if not exactly *wreathed in smiles*,

betrayed and broken-hearted as he is,
he's learnt that he must be not only vigilant

but also, and in spite of everything,
cheerful till he's blue in the face.

His Bushy Hair

This nice young girl who's come to cut his hair
might as well go home – he's much too busy

discovering, or trying to discover,
bushy hair or not, the end of time.

His Mugs of Coffee

Although the mugs of Maxwell House coffee,
the Garibaldi biscuits and the florentines

brighten up his days *to some extent*,
they neither will nor can keep at bay

this feeling that there's something wrong, that something,
however small, has not yet been addressed.

His Sticky Florentine

The blue-and-yellow coffee-stained mug
draining on the stainless-steel draining-board
with CHAMPION CHAMPION peeling off the side
still retains the warmth of its owner,
now resting in the chair his Other Half
seemed to spend her life in, fast asleep;
and shouldn't he, he's thinking to himself,
in this bitter weather, leave the chair
and pull the heavy curtain round the door,
(curtain or, strictly speaking, blanket)
and as he toys with what to call the colour,
apple-green, perhaps, he hears a knock

he hopes and prays is not a certain vagabond
who shouldn't be allowed to roam the streets
and frighten people in their own homes,
but when the knocking reasserts itself
he creeps across the carpet to the door,
intending to unlock it and to open it
just a tiny crack, when it stops;
he turns and makes his way to the florentine,
the sticky, chilled, half-eaten cherry florentine
wrapped in greaseproof-paper in the fridge;
and after he has finished it he plunges
his sticky little face into a bucket.

ORNAMENTAL LAKES
AS SEEN FROM TRAINS

Silence is sometimes yellow.

Sandy Hollows, Godless Pines

Sandy hollows, godless pines. A man
blinded by the sun, by the sand,

blinded by my furious orange face –
as orange and as furious as the sun

if the sun had never learnt to set –
is failing to look me in the eye.

The Pit of His Stomach

He's like a man whose body crawls with flies,
they crawl inside his ears and down his throat

and down into the pit of his stomach –
thousands of them milling about

and making it impossible to hear
anything that anybody's saying.

His Eyes

The man I must not touch on pain of death
walks across the grass like a doll.

His arms and legs are stiff, his eyes are blank –
or, rather, they appear to be blank

but if we look again we will see
the sorrow he must never know we know about.

Californian Waffles

Toffee-coloured, toffee-coloured, toffee-coloured,
everything about him is toffee-coloured –

the tan, the cat, the gloves, the leather wallet,
the toffee-coloured, toffee-nosed face

he longs to cram with warm and very sticky
toffee-coloured Californian waffles.

Warmth

Same old thing. Fear of being touched.
Fear of being brushed against; of eating;
fear of someone saying to someone else

something someone else will soon regret;
fear of being cuddled, fear of gloves,
fear of being naked, fear of coats,

fear of being cold, of being warm,
of being wrapped or trampled on by warmth,
fear of warmth. By *warmth* I mean warmth.

His Hand

The hand he's holding out to me's so clean
the way it gleams can seem almost brutal.

Man on a Lawn

The sun is shining brightly when the man
steps onto the lawn like a mannequin

who wants to very much but who can't
find himself bursting into tears.

Chickens

Even when he's kind I feel like chicken-shit
shat by chickens out beheading worms.
And when he isn't? Like the headless worm.

The Height

The height, the charm, the jutting chin, the cheekbones,
the piercing eyes – what more could he want?

He doesn't know. It's wearing him down.
He needs to know. He needs to know everything.

The Golden Pennies

Melancholy, moisturised, we sit
and watch the golden pennies pile up

and mock the questions I will never ask
because I am afraid of the answers.

You Either Love a Person or You Don't

I step onto his shoes and cling on tight,
my face between his knees, but the man

shakes me off and kicks me in the hedge.
I'm three years old. The man is my father.

You either love a person or you don't.
That's what I've been told but it's not true.

Sauerkraut

It's something like a sin made of sauerkraut
but what that something is I've no idea

and when he waves his hand in my direction –
his surprisingly child-like hand – I wave back

but in a most unnatural-looking way
like someone trying to free themselves from a wetsuit.

Chicken Thigh

The awkward question, like a chicken thigh
sitting in the fridge on a plate

in a sort of green and lonely glow,
is getting more awkward by the minute.

Windowpane

Something cold and thin, like a windowpane,
is thickening, inch by inch, between us,

him on one side, me the other, waiting
to see how long it takes to be unbearable.

The Eerie Llama

Like the long-legged man inside my head,
the long-legged ghost who's unpredictable

in everything except his pertinacity,
the eerie llama glides along his fence.

The Chair

I want to sit him down and tell him everything.
What is there to be afraid of? Nothing.

But do I 'tell him everything'? I don't.
I only tell him very simple things.

My Horse-hoof Soup

His face is thin and grey like the soup
that shudders at the sound of galloping horsemen,

his throat is like the pines where the birds,
the flocks of tiny birds you can't see,

are stabbing at the panic-stricken beetles.
I try to take a sip but it's impossible.

Castle

It used to be such fun being loved
but now it isn't fun, it's like a castle

where strangers that I do my best to follow
do their best to help me not get lost

but when they find they can't they get discouraged
and wander off into another room.

Fear of Coffee

Fear of coffee, fear of tall buildings,
fear of people asking how I am;

fear of the embraces of bereavement counsellors,
fear of babies who are grown men;

fear of sitting next to him at tables
where neighbours squeeze their blobs of mayonnaise.

Wedding Cake

So tall, so bored, so irresistible,
he's not so much a man as a wedding cake –

a wedding cake that deep inside its icing
is concentrating on not thinking *knife*.

The Tank

He peers at me as if I'm in a tank.
He marvels at my ugliness and stupor.

I can be as ugly as I like.
Better to be ugly than afraid.

Bitter Chocolates on a Silver Tray

His hair is long and gold like golden syrup.
He brings me chocolates on a silver tray.

I'm begging him to listen but he doesn't.
He doesn't listen to a word I say.

Why? Because it doesn't make sense.
Not to him, not to anyone.

The Mourner

I wish he'd either never been born
or die – and free me to relax and mourn,

'relax' because I'll feel safe at last
and 'mourn' because to mourn changes everything.

Why I Love Gyrocopters

I love the way they let me be a bird
face to face with nothing but the sky.

I love the word itself – the edgy 'pt',
the 'cop' of 'cop', the 'cop' of Copenhagen,

Copenhagen where the boots were made
he took time off to fly to to try on.

Another reason – well, the main reason:
my mother told me only men can fly.

The Tall Man

If I want to tell the tall man
not to be unkind to me, I can;

I can try and help him to relax.
Another option is to murder him.

One Morning in July

I'm standing in the mud, knee-deep in cabbages,
when, much to my surprise, I see him wave –

as if I am the woman he'll remember
when everybody else has been forgotten;

as if he is no longer ashamed,
ablaze among the cabbages, of hope;

as if it doesn't matter that his hands,
once as clean as yachts, will be ruined.

Ornamental Lakes as Seen from Trains

I might as well have been afraid of milk,
of ornamental lakes as seen from trains;

as boxes of milk-chocolate chocolate rabbits.
To be afraid is just a waste of time.

SHOEBILL

Elbow

Huddled in your bed, I watch your elbow
slowly bend and straighten as you paint

until the sleeping pills you have given me
slowly but surely take effect

and all night long I sleep without moving
like a shoebill underneath a coat.

Snowdrop

You love me like a man loves a snowdrop
whose love the frail snowdrop can't withstand.

You love me like a man loves a bird
on whose white foot he slips a tiny ring.

Hare

I'm lying on your bed like a hare
lying injured on a mountainside

and listening to the sound of the snow
steadily filling the valley.

It's Like a Dream

It's like a dream. It's just the two of us.
When visitors arrive I go to sleep

and let them smoke, play records and have sex.
And when they've gone you feed me chocolate rabbits.

Pig

I wear the same black dress every day.
On top of that I wear a black coat

in which you hide the tiny rubber pig
you give me every week because you love me.

Bird

I'm ugly, lazy, dirty and won't move.
Every single thing is too much trouble.

I hide in bed all day like a bird
that's got no wings; that he's reduced to feeding.

The Wall

While you're quietly having sex with someone
I'm dreaming in my corner by the wall

of being someone's dormouse – someone holy
having sex ten thousand years too late.

The Edge of Town

To get to it we have to walk for hours,
in shoes like slippers, to the edge of town –

returning, hand in sticky hand, at dawn
across a land of glass and yellow dogshit.

Mole

You love me like the field loves the mole
that makes its home among the flints and roots,

building tunnels only moles can navigate,
tunnels I increasingly get lost in.

Watcher

I watch you from the bed as you work,
perched before your easel with your back to me.

If my body moves, you purse your lips.
Sometimes you will turn, sometimes not.

When you turn I watch your long hair
changing shape like water underwater.

You Hold Me in Your Lap

You love me more than ever but it's hard
because I am too ill to understand.

You hold me in your lap like a mountain
holds a snow-encrusted mountain hare.

Your Hair Against My Back

Your hair against my back is cold and thin.
Your body is uncomfortable and bony.

Sleeping here beside you is like home;
like sleeping in a cutlery drawer.

Fish

When you come to feed me when it's feeding time,
I nibble your blue fingertips like fish

that, nibbling the surface of their water,
graze their silver lips against thin air.

Skinny as a Rake

You're skinny as a rake; you don't sleep;
you can't go out; you eat like a bird

and even when you're wide awake you're dreaming
your magical but heartbreaking dreams.

Sandbag

Beginnings are so simple but you're finding
that, even if you want to, you now can't

dislodge me from the bed where, like a sandbag,
I fill whatever space there is with fear.

Ugly

I may be ugly but I don't care.
Actually I don't even know.

I lie in bed surrendering myself
to being loved by nothing but a coat.

Like the Flightless Birds

Like the flightless birds that roamed the earth
thousands of years ago, I can't talk;

and if I try to walk I just fall over
through air that smells of Germolene and turpentine.

Goblin

You work away all day like a goblin –
sweeping, sewing, stabbing at your paints –

and as you work you never forget
the coat behind you rising and falling.

The Love of Your Life

You love me like the love of your life.
On summer nights you peek inside my brain

to watch my hosts of extraterrestrial grasshoppers
crushed together learning not to sing.

Mice

All you want to do is go to bed,
go to bed and sleep like a baby,

that's all you want to do but your eyes
never stop peering at the canvases

where hour after hour your tiny brushes
pick their way across the size like mice.

The Coat

O how can you lie down when your skin
never stops itching and the radio

plays the wrong music and your bed
is occupied by someone in a coat

who stubbornly refuses to let go of it,
who rolls herself inside it like a ball

if anybody tries to take her hand
and lead her step by step to the door?

Hands

Together we are travelling to the hospital.
You hold my hand all the way there.

Your kindness encloses me like ice,
preventing me from falling apart.

The Hospital in Winter

The hospital overlooks a lake
that creaks, as if with longing – but a lake

doesn't even know what longing is!
On the seventh floor the young doctor

has never been alone with a woman
he cares about so little, if at all.

Cats with Spots

I fill the bath with dressing-gowns and towels,
quickly turn the light off, and climb in.

Cats have spots but not as bad as mine.
Mine are on the inside not the outside.

The doctor recommends masturbation.
I can think of nothing less appealing.

Suitcase

You think you can get over it, but no,
there I sit, day after day,

like a little crocodile-skin suitcase
begging you not to leave me there.

Your Beautiful Long Hair

You bring me chocolate eggs and chocolate oranges
and offer them politely to the nurses

and chat to them about the television programmes
I haven't watched for millions of years.

I'm sitting in the day-room with my eyes shut.
They can't believe how sweet to me you are.

I'm always dressed in black from head to foot
and never speak, not even to you.

When you turn and walk away they gasp
in wonder at the beauty of your hair.

You Tell Me That You Love Me

You tell me that you love me very much.
I never say a word. I never do.

You tell me you will love me for ever.
I never even open my eyes.

You tell me if I kill myself, I kill myself.
You tell me it won't make *the slightest difference*.

The House

In the dream in which I'm blindly running
this way, that way, like a lost sheep

trapped inside a house, the house is him.
To disagree is out of the question.

The Moth at Night

You hold me in your arms like the night
in which the moth can hunt but cannot love,

it cannot love but as it hunts its heartbeat
deepens the silence they share.

Cake

Today they are explaining what will happen:
your visits will be every *other* day.

The doctors see how thin you are. They see
the way you won't let go of my hand.

The doctors are begging you to leave.
And now the matron in her tight dress

reappears, carrying a cake
and telling you to eat it, and to rest.

Bedside-locker Pig Farm

Some of them haven't got heads
but all of them are as hard as nails.

Late at night when everyone's asleep
I listen to them rootling about.

Frosty Weather

As you work you pray – like a thief
hanging on a cross in frosty weather.

You pray with such devotion and tenacity
that when I say you pray I mean hallucinate.

Dot

I do not know you love me but I will.
Later, when I'm better, I will see

what I cannot see when I am ill
and shrinking into nothing like a dot.

Summertime

You paint all night. At dawn you stand up
and start the long cold walk to the hospital.

You haven't seen your family for years.
You haven't even told them where you live.

You live so far away that, for them,
when it's winter here, for them it's summertime.